Biographies That Build Character

Author   Kathy Rogers

Editor   Kathy Rogers

Illustrator   Elizabeth Adams Marks

Page

Curriculum and Character Education 2

Traits of Good Character 3

Story Activities 4

Courage

    Jackie Robinson 5

    Eleanor Roosevelt 8

Citizenship

    Thomas Jefferson 11

    Andrew Carnegie 14

Responsibility

    Booker T. Washington 17

    Albert Schweitzer 20

Loyalty

    Abigail Adams 23

    Robert E. Lee 26

Perseverance

    Mohandas Gandhi 29

    Albert Einstein 32

Page

Honesty

    Sitting Bull 35

    George Washington 38

Respect

    John Muir .41

    Martin Luther King, Jr. 44

Trustworthiness

    Sacagawea 47

    Abraham Lincoln 50

Fairness

    Cesar Chavez 53

    Frederick Douglass 56

Caring

    Dorothea Dix 59

    Mother Teresa 62

EP343 • ©2001 Edupress, Inc. • P.O. Box 883 • Dana Point, CA 92629

www.edupressinc.com

ISBN 1-56472-343-7

Printed in USA

Curriculum and Character Education

Across the nation, character education programs have become an integral part of the curriculum. Schools are actively developing programs to help students understand and develop commonly held ethical values and characteristics. Now you can link the development of good character to a standards-based, language arts curriculum.

The activities in *Biographies That Build Character* will not only enhance students' reading and writing skills, it will develop their understanding and appreciation of the basic principles of good character. Increased awareness will be exhibited in the development of students' life skills in:

- Expressive and receptive communication skills, conflict resolution
- Coping with difficulties, recognizing boundaries, being flexible, maintaining perspective, being resilient, and deferring impulses
- Critical thinking, problem-solving, decision-making
- Anger management
- Courtesy, sharing, good manners, mutual respect, civility, and graciousness
- Insight, self-reflection, self-discipline, self-worth, self-respect, self-awareness, self-reliance, and self-management
- Relationship building within the family, in a work or school environment, between friends, and in the community
- Organization, leadership, time management, goal setting, work ethic, and accountability
- Appreciation of the differences among people
- Citizenship and civic responsibility
- Prevention of violence

About the Book

Biographies about historical figures are important tools in the teaching of character education. Many of the people discussed in this book will be familiar to students. These biographies are intended to help students recognize how the personal traits of these people contributed to their influence and success.

How to Use the Book

Biographies That Build Character is divided into ten sections, one for each of the characteristics addressed. Each section contains two units which each contain an introductory page, a one-page biography, and a reproducible worksheet.

The introductory page of each unit is written to the teacher and includes these elements:

- Summary—A brief synopsis of the biography.
- Concepts to Consider—Suggestions for introducing the unit to the students.
- Discussion Topics—Specific topics related to the biography, encouraging the students to think further about the subject.
- Writing Activity—An introduction to the worksheet.

The biography page and the worksheet are designed to be reproduced for student use.

Additional suggestions for extended use of the story activities are found on page 4.

Traits of Good Character

For the purpose of this book, we have selected ten characteristics that are generally :epted as traits of good character: perseverance, respect, courage, trustworthiness, :zenship, fairness, responsibility, caring, honesty, and loyalty. The definition of each of these iracter traits is listed below, along with related traits that may be found in the teaching character education.

❖ **Perseverance**—Perseverance is the willingness to make a continuing, patient effort at getting something accomplished. Related traits are persistence and working hard.

❖ **Respect**—Respect is a regard for the worth of someone or something. Respect includes respect for oneself, for the rights and dignity of other people, for laws and authority, and for the environment. Related traits are appreciation, understanding, and esteem.

❖ **Courage**—Courage is the state of being fearless, unafraid, and brave. A person with courage is willing to face and deal with danger, trouble, or pain. Related traits are bravery and fortitude.

❖ **Trustworthiness**—Trustworthiness is being deserving of trust. A trustworthy person is honest and can be depended upon. Related traits are promise-keeping and reliability.

❖ **Citizenship**—Citizenship is the conduct or behavior of a person in relation to the group in which he lives. A good citizen is respectful of the rights, duties, and privileges of all citizens. Related traits are cooperativeness, fairness, and neighborliness.

❖ **Fairness**—Fairness is the ability to makes decisions and judgments that are honest and impartial. A person who is fair is not influenced by self-interest, prejudice, or favoritism. Related traits are good sportsmanship and open-mindedness.

❖ **Responsibility**—Responsibility is being accountable for actions and circumstances that are within a person's control. A responsible person takes care of himself and others, and fulfills his obligations. Related traits are self-discipline, dependability, and reliability.

❖ **Caring**—Caring is an expression of love or regard. A person who is caring shows concern for other people. Related traits are compassion, understanding, empathy, consideration, and sympathy.

❖ **Honesty**—Honesty means being truthful and upright. An honest person does not lie, cheat, or steal. Related traits are truthfulness and integrity.

❖ **Loyalty**—Loyalty is the quality of being faithful to one's country, family, friends, duties, or beliefs. A loyal person follows through on his promises and commitments. Related traits are friendship and fidelity.

Story Activities

Class Debate

After reading and discussing the biography, choose teams and hold a classroom debate. Defend your opinions about the moral issues faced by the person and his or her behavior.

On Stage

Rewrite the biography as a play, and perform the play for your classmates or for another class.

Character Ed Bulletin Board

Display the biographies and finished worksheets on a Character Ed bulletin board for "Back to School" night or Open House.

Write and Illustrate

Rewrite the biography in picture book format. Illustrate your book with crayons or markers.

Jackie Robinson
Courage

Summary

Jackie Robinson was subjected to bigotry and racism when he signed on to play major league baseball. His courage helped him to resist the urge to fight back, and his dignity earned him the respect of the fans and other players.

Concepts to Consider

Individuals exhibit courage not only by what they do, but by what they choose not to do. It is very difficult to control one's behavior when provoked by the cruel actions of others. Jackie Robinson's ability to withstand the prejudices of the people around him was a benefit not only to himself, but to other people who were trying to end segregation. He was also an example to other Blacks who were struggling to succeed in a segregated world.

In order to understand the importance of what Robinson accomplished, it is necessary that students understand just how extensive the effects of segregation could be. Conduct a class discussion to explore the topic. Discuss the purpose of the NAACP, and explore what the students already know about the civil rights movement.

Extended Responses

Discussion Topics

Objective: Students will examine the issue of segregation and think about how segregation might impact the life of an individual.

- Using a dictionary, define the word "segregation." Restate the definition in your own words. Give examples of segregation.

- What questions would you ask in an interview with Jackie Robinson about the difficulties he faced during his baseball career?

- Evaluate the significance of Jackie Robinson's success.

Writing Activity—Page 7

Objective: Students will summarize the experiences of Jackie Robinson and create a Courage Hall of Fame award that recognizes his courage.

Jackie Robinson was inducted into the Baseball Hall of Fame in 1962. His success at making a place for himself in the white baseball world and his dedication to the civil rights movement would certainly make him a candidate for a Courage Hall of Fame.

The worksheet is an award for the Courage Hall of Fame. Students are asked to write two paragraphs explaining why Jackie Robinson deserves to be recognized for his courage. Encourage students to use specific examples from his life in their writing. If possible, provide additional resource materials for students to use.

Jackie Robinson
Courage

In 1947, Jackie Robinson became the first black American to play major league baseball. Until that day, Blacks could only play in black baseball leagues. It took a tremendous amount of courage for him to step out onto Ebbets Field in New York for the first time. That step was just the beginning.

Jack Roosevelt Robinson was born near Cairo, Georgia, on January 31, 1919. He had four older brothers and sisters. His father was a sharecropper. When Jackie was still very young, his father left the family. His mother then moved them all to Pasadena, California, to find work.

In high school and junior college, Jackie excelled in football, basketball, baseball, and track. He earned a scholarship to UCLA. There, he became the first UCLA athlete to earn varsity letters in four sports. When Pearl Harbor was bombed he enlisted in the Army, earning a commission as Second Lieutenant. In 1944, Robinson faced a court-martial for refusing to move to the rear of an army bus. He was cleared of all charges and received an honorable discharge.

Jackie Robinson joined professional baseball in the spring of 1945 with the Negro American League. In August he met with Branch Rickey, owner of the Brooklyn Dodgers. Rickey had been searching for a black ball player that could withstand the pressure of being the first black man in the major leagues.

Rickey was very honest with Robinson. "Do you have the guts not to fight back?" he asked. He warned Jackie that he would succeed only if he did not respond to the cruelties that people would dish out. Jackie signed on to play for a year with the Dodgers' farm team, and then for the Dodgers.

Playing for the major leagues was just as hard as Rickey promised. Players on rival teams were hostile. Pitchers would throw balls right at Jackie, forcing him to "hit the dirt." Insults flew from other players as well as fans in the stands. Players on his own team threatened to go on strike if he was allowed to play. When the team traveled, Jackie was not allowed to stay in the same hotel as the rest of his team. There were many restaurants that he was not allowed to enter.

Jackie Robinson had the courage to withstand it all. He never lost his temper, no matter how he was provoked. He earned the respect of his teammates and many fans, and was selected the league's Rookie of the Year. In ten years he appeared in six All-Star games and six World Series. He was elected to the Baseball Hall of Fame in 1962.

Robinson went on to be a successful banker, and was active in the NAACP and the civil rights movement. His courage and perseverance have been an inspiration to athletes of all races and colors.

COURAGE HALL OF FAME

JACKIE ROBINSON

_____

_____

_____

_____

_____

_____

_____

_____

_____

_____

_____

_____

_____

_____

_____

_____

_____

_____

_____

_____

_____

Instructions:

Write at least two paragraphs to explain why Jackie Robinson deserves to be in the Courage Hall of Fame. Use examples from his life story in your writing.

Eleanor Roosevelt
Courage

Summary

Eleanor Roosevelt overcame her shy, private nature to become one of the most influential women in the world.

Concepts to Consider

During the early part of her life, Eleanor Roosevelt was plagued with the sense of being unworthy and unloved. After her marriage, she was overshadowed by a domineering mother-in-law and a husband with a flair for politics.

A loving, caring person, Eleanor found happiness in serving other people. Before her marriage, she worked in a New York settlement house trying to help people better themselves. After marriage, she devoted herself to her husband and children. Her desire to keep her husband active drove her to be involved in politics in a way that no other woman had done before. Once she found herself in the public arena, she strove to do as much as she could to make people's lives better.

Extended Responses

Discussion Topics

Objective: Students will recognize some of the difficulties Eleanor faced as a child and learn about some of the issues that were important to her.

- Name some of the influences that may have made Eleanor withdrawn as a child.

- Eleanor Roosevelt was the first First Lady to give interviews for the press. What reasons do you think she had for doing this? What questions do you think reporters asked her?

- Eleanor was a supporter of the civil rights movement and the women's rights movement. Make a list of information you have about these two issues.

Writing Activity—Page 10

Objective: Students will be introduced to the Universal Declaration of Human Rights, the United Nations' statement about the rights of all people, and will write an essay explaining the first article of the Declaration.

Eleanor Roosevelt considered her work with the United Nations to be some of the most important work she ever did. She was instrumental in the creation of the Universal Declaration of Human Rights, outlining the basic rights of every person living in the world. This statement expressed her own personal feelings about human rights.

The worksheet "Human Rights for All" introduces Article 1 of the Declaration, and asks students to write an essay exploring the meaning of the Article.

Eleanor Roosevelt
Courage

Eleanor Roosevelt once said, "You gain strength, courage and confidence by every experience in which you really stop to look fear in the face…" Facing her fears was something that Mrs. Roosevelt did all of her life.

Eleanor was the daughter of an alcoholic father and an aloof mother who was disappointed because Eleanor wasn't pretty. Eleanor was insecure and shy, and in her own words, "always afraid of something." Marriage to her distant cousin, Franklin Roosevelt, years of childbearing, and living under the influence of her mother-in-law increased her insecurity. After 13 years of marriage, problems developed between Eleanor and Franklin, and Eleanor decided she had to find interests outside her family.

When Franklin entered politics, Eleanor became his political helpmate. Although public appearances and social gatherings were agonizing, she knew that her presence was important. It became even more important when Franklin was struck with polio and became paralyzed from the waist down. In order to keep him interested in politics, Eleanor became an active participant in his political career, being his "eyes and ears." Franklin was elected governor of New York in 1928, and from that point until the day he died, Eleanor traveled the nation and the world in his place. Terrified of public speaking, she learned to make speeches that were to the point and well received. She made friends in the political world, and was one of a group of women who were becoming politically influential.

Franklin Roosevelt was elected President during the Great Depression. As First Lady, Eleanor visited slums, sharecropper's homes, and coal mines to be able to tell her husband firsthand of what conditions many American people were facing. She was the first First Lady to grant press interviews. She gave lectures and wrote a daily syndicated newspaper column. During World War II, she visited servicemen at the war front. Vitally interested in women's rights and the civil rights movement, Eleanor became a powerful advocate for disadvantaged people in America.

When Franklin Roosevelt died at the beginning of his fourth term, Eleanor thought her time of influence was finished. But President Harry Truman asked her to be a delegate to the newly formed United Nations, a project that was dear to her husband. In that role, she spoke out for the human rights of people throughout the world. Until the time of her death, Eleanor traveled the world, learning about people and extending help and hope to all of those that she could. She had come a long way from the timid child she had been.

Human Rights for All

On December 10, 1948, the General Assembly of the United Nations adopted the Universal Declaration of Human Rights. This was their statement of how they believed all human beings should be treated, and it was their hope that these principles would be taught to students all over the world.

Read Article 1 of the Declaration, written below. Write an essay that explains what the article means.

Article 1

All human beings are born free and equal in dignity and rights. They are endowed with reason and conscience and should act towards one another in a spirit of brotherhood.

Thomas Jefferson
Citizenship

Summary

Thomas Jefferson, author of the Declaration of Independence, was a supporter of the natural rights of all people. His beliefs were the cornerstone on which the new American government was built.

Concepts to Consider

During the American Revolution, there were many personalities involved in the fight for independence and the creation of a new government. Individuals stand out for specific roles and events: George Washington for his military leadership and role as first President, Patrick Henry for his "give me liberty or give me death" speech. Benjamin Franklin is remembered for his talent in diplomacy.

Thomas Jefferson is famous for writing the Declaration of Independence. But the true significance of his role is how his beliefs helped shape the ideals that form the basis of our nation's government. His belief in the natural rights of all people and his trust in their ability to govern themselves shaped the United States Constitution and Bill of Rights.

Extended Responses

Discussion Topics

Objective: Students will examine some of the beliefs of Thomas Jefferson and recognize how they influenced the shaping of the new nation.

- Jefferson's early work in the Virginia House of Burgesses involved the removal of *primogeniture* and *entailment* in land ownership. Use a dictionary to define these terms.

- Removing laws regarding primogeniture and entailment meant that more people could vote. Explain why that is true. How does his belief in these laws reflect his beliefs about the ability of people to govern themselves?

- Thomas Jefferson owned slaves, but he thought that slavery was an evil institution. He did not try to end slavery because he felt that it was not the right time. List reasons he might have thought the time was too early.

Writing Activity—Page 13

Objective: Students will read sections of the Declaration of Independence and explain how they relate to Jefferson's beliefs.

The Declaration of Independence expressed the colonists' reasons for proclaiming their freedom from Great Britain.

The following worksheet contains sections of the Declaration of Independence. Students will read the sections and write their ideas about how each section relates to Thomas Jefferson's beliefs in the natural rights of all people.

© EDUPRESS, INC.   EP343

Thomas Jefferson
Citizenship

The inscription on Thomas Jefferson's tombstone reads, "Author of the Declaration of American Independence, of the Statute of Virginia for religious freedom, and Father of the University of Virginia." All of these accomplishments were more important to Jefferson than his two terms as President.

Thomas Jefferson was born on April 13, 1743, in Albemarle County, Virginia. His father was a planter and surveyor. His mother's family was one of the oldest families in Virginia. Jefferson studied at the College of William and Mary. He then studied law. He married Martha Wayles Skelton in 1772. They had six children, but only two lived past childhood. They lived at Monticello, the home that Jefferson designed and built near Shadwell, Virginia. Martha died in 1782.

Jefferson never thought of himself as a professional politician. Instead, he regarded himself as a public-spirited citizen and a practical thinker. He believed that people could govern themselves, and felt that government should involve itself in the lives of people as little as possible. He loved liberty in every form, and worked for freedom of speech, press, religion, and other civil liberties.

Jefferson was not an eloquent speaker, but he was a talented, clear writer. He was a leading member of the Continental Congress, and wrote the Declaration of Independence. The Declaration affirmed belief in the natural rights of all people, and was an expression of the American mind.

Jefferson returned to Virginia to begin a campaign of social reform. Jefferson sponsored bills to end the practice of primogeniture and entailment, giving voting rights to more of the state's citizens. He believed that "aristocracy by wealth" was less important than "acristocracy of virtue and talent." Jefferson also introduced bills that ensured religious tolerance. He returned to serve in the national government first as a Congressman, then as minister to France and secretary of state. He served as Vice President under George Washington and John Adams. In 1801, he began his first term as President. Jefferson's two terms saw the expansion of the nation and the explorations of Lewis and Clark. His style of governing reflected his feelings about the dignity of individuals: he began the practice of people shaking hands with the President rather than bowing.

Jefferson retired from politics in 1809 and returned to Monticello. In his later years he worked tirelessly to create the University of Virginia, which opened in 1825. Presidents James Madison and James Monroe consulted him frequently on public affairs. When he died on July 4, 1826, it could be said that Jefferson had molded the American spirit and mind. Every American generation has looked back to him for guidance and inspiration.

A Statement of Belief

The final draft of the Declaration of Independence was adopted on July 4, 1776. In many ways, the final document was a statement of Thomas Jefferson's beliefs in the natural rights of all people. Read each of the sections of the Declaration below. Below each section, explain how that section is a statement of Jefferson's beliefs.

———<◆>———

We hold these truths to be self-evident, that all men are created equal, that they are endowed by their Creator with certain unalienable Rights, that among these are Life, Liberty and the pursuit of Happiness.

———<◆>———

That to secure these rights, Governments are instituted among Men, deriving their just powers from the consent of the governed,

———<◆>———

That whenever any Form of Government becomes destructive of these ends, it is the Right of the People to alter or to abolish it, and to institute new Government, laying its foundation on such principles and organizing its powers in such form, as to them shall seem most likely to effect their Safety and Happiness.

———<◆>———

But when a long train of abuses and usurpations, pursuing invariably the same Object evinces a design to reduce them under absolute Despotism, it is their right, it is their duty, to throw off such Government, and to provide new Guards for their future security.

Andrew Carnegie
Citizenship

Summary

Andrew Carnegie, once considered the richest man in the word, used his wealth to benefit other people. He did not believe in charity, but he did believe that the wealthy had a responsibility to help people help themselves.

Concepts to Consider

Public libraries have an important place in today's society. The majority of children in the United States have easy access to books, free of charge. They probably give little thought to what their lives would be like if books were not readily available to them.

Take time to discuss how students use the public library: research, entertainment, special programs. How many students use the library instead of purchasing books? How would their lives change if they had to purchase books rather than borrow? What impact would there be on people who did not have money to buy books?

Extended Responses

Discussion Topics

Objective: Students will examine the concepts of "charity" and "helping people to help themselves." They will identify ways in which people can help others.

• Compare the concepts of charity and "helping people to help themselves."

• Brainstorm a list of problems that people face in our society today. Select one of the problems and propose ways to help. Categorize the suggestions based on whether they are "charity" or "helping people to help themselves."

Writing Activity—Page 16

Objective: Students will summarize the heroic behavior of another person, and recognize the contribution that person has made to the lives of other people.

Andrew Carnegie had this inscribed on the tombstone of a 17-year old boy who drowned during a rescue attempt: "The false heroes of barbarous man are those who can only boast of the destruction of their fellows. The true heroes of civilizations are those alone who save or greatly serve them."

This act of heroism and the deadly rescue attempts of two men in a mine explosion in 1904 moved Carnegie to establish the Carnegie Hero Fund Commission, an organization dedicated to helping people who are injured in heroic acts or helping their survivors. For complete information about the award and qualifications, write to the Commission or visit their website at *carnegiehero.org*

The worksheet "My Hero" asks students to recall a heroic act they have read or heard about, and to write a letter applying for help for that hero. They will outline why they think their hero deserves recognition, acknowledging that person's contribution to the lives of others.

Andrew Carnegie
Citizenship

When Andrew Carnegie sold the Carnegie Steel Company in 1901, he became the richest man in the world. Even though he was still wealthy at the time of his death in 1919, he succeeded in giving 90% of his fortune away to improve the lives of the people around him.

Andrew Carnegie was born in Dunfermline, Scotland, in 1835. His father was a weaver. In 1848, the Carnegie family immigrated to the United States, settling in what is now Pittsburgh, Pennsylvania. Andrew worked hard helping to support his family, first at menial jobs, but always working toward better jobs. His industry and good investment sense helped him gain tremendous wealth. He became a leading steel manufacturer. In 1901, his estimated wealth was $500 million. He married in 1896, and had one daughter, Margaret, born in 1897.

Andrew Carnegie believed strongly in what he called the "Gospel of Wealth." He felt that in any capitalistic society, there would always be a few people that would control most of the money. It was the responsibility of those few to use their money for the benefit of the rest of society. Carnegie's personal goal was to give most of his money away before he was 35 years old. Carnegie also believed that education was the key to success.

Carnegie used his money in many ways. He was part of a group that wanted to simplify spelling. He established the Carnegie Institution to fund research in American colleges, the Carnegie Endowment for International Peace, and the Carnegie Corporation for scientific research. He gave money for museums and concert halls, such as Carnegie Hall in New York City. He started the Carnegie Institute of Technology in Pittsburgh, which is now Carnegie Mellon University. Many of Carnegie's endowments are still fruitful today, contributing to scientific research and even children's educational television.

Andrew Carnegie's most notable contribution was in public libraries. In all, he gave money to establish more than 2,500 libraries throughout the world. He believed in the value of libraries for two purposes. First, Carnegie believed that every person should have the opportunity to read in an effort to become educated. As a boy he worked long hours to help his family, leaving him no time for school. A man named Colonel Anderson had a library of books that he lent to boys. This was the basis of Andrew's education, and he was grateful to the Colonel his entire life. Carnegie libraries were a tribute to the Colonel. The second purpose for the Carnegie libraries was for the cultural education of immigrants. Andrew believed immigrants would use the library like he had and as a result would be able to make better contributions to American society. Carnegie believed that his money should go to benefit the society in which he lived.

My Hero

The Carnegie Hero Fund Commission grants monetary awards to a person "who voluntarily risks his or her life, knowingly, to an extraordinary degree while saving or attempting to save the life of another person."

Think about events you know of in your own life, or look through the newspaper for an interesting story, selecting a person you think might qualify for this award. In the form below, write a letter to the Commission, explaining what this person did and why you feel he or she deserves to be recognized.

Carnegie Hero Fund Commission
425 6th Avenue, Suite 1640
Pittsburgh, PA 15219-1823

Gentlemen:

Sincerely,

Booker T. Washington
Responsibility

Summary

Booker T. Washington, born a slave, struggled to secure an education for himself, believing that education was the key to a successful life. He opened and operated the Tuskegee Normal & Industrial Institute, founded on the idea that education would help freed Blacks find jobs and gain financial security.

Concepts to Consider

After the Civil War, many former slaves were left with no means of supporting themselves. Despite hardships they suffered, slaves were not faced with issues like providing their own food or securing a home for themselves. When they were emancipated, they were forced into a world where they had to find a way to make a living.

Booker T. Washington felt that helping these people find a way to make a living and to build self-sufficient lives was more important than demanding political equality. He believed that once they were financially self-sufficient, the rest of society would accept them more readily and that political equality would follow.

Extended Responses

Discussion Topics

Objective: Students will understand the concept of being responsible for oneself in terms of Washington's belief in practical education.

• Identify problems that freed slaves might have faced after their emancipation.

• Booker T. Washington believed that teaching people a trade (practical education) would help them to take responsibility for their own futures. Debate the pros and cons of this issue.

• Propose ways in which you can be responsible for yourself.

Writing Activity—Page 19

Objective: Students will evaluate the key points of the opposing views of Booker T. Washington and his contemporary, W.E.B. Du Bois, an African American writer and activist.

W.E.B. Du Bois criticized Booker T. Washington's beliefs. While Washington advised Blacks to accept their position in society, Du Bois said the fight for equality could not wait. Washington thought Blacks should learn practical work skills, while Du Bois believed that talented black people should be able to attend college and become leaders.

On the worksheet "The Quest for Equality" students are asked to list the main points of the position of each man, especially regarding education. They are then asked to write a paragraph explaining which view they believe is the more valid.

Booker T. Washington
Responsibility

Booker T. Washington rose up from slavery and illiteracy to become the foremost educator and leader of black Americans at the turn of the century. Washington's childhood was one of poverty, slavery, and backbreaking work. He was born a slave in 1856. His mother, Jane, raised him, and he was put to work as early as possible. Since it was illegal for a slave to learn to read and write, Washington received no education.

At the end of the Civil War in 1865, Washington's stepfather found work packing salt in Malden, West Virginia. Jane moved herself and her children to join her husband. The nine-year-old Washington spent exhausting days packing salt. Like many Blacks after the Emancipation, Washington wanted an education. Despite the exhausting days, he used his free time to go to school. When he was 16 he decided that he wanted to go to Hampton Institute in Virginia. At Hampton he was trained as a teacher, and after graduation he returned to Hampton to teach.

Booker quickly absorbed the philosophy of Hampton's founder, General Samuel Chapman Armstrong. Armstrong believed in work, study, hygiene, morality, self-discipline, and self-reliance. He also believed that in addition to an education students should receive training in a trade. This type of discipline, Booker realized, would help newly-freed Blacks find their place in the world. He recognized that former slaves were not equipped to go into the free, working world. They were not used to having to earn a living just to provide themselves with a home and food. When Armstrong recommended Washington as principal of a new school—Tuskegee Normal School in Tuskegee, Alabama—Washington found his opportunity to help other Blacks.

The new school opened on July 4, 1881. The school taught specific trades such as carpentry, farming, and mechanics. It also specialized in training teachers. In time, Tuskegee Normal School was renamed Tuskegee Institute, and eventually Tuskegee University. It became famous as a model of industrial education. By acquiring practical work skills, Blacks would be able to find financial stability.

Booker T. Washington did not think that Blacks should demand equal rights. He believed that as blacks improved their economic position, they would be given civil and political rights. He urged blacks to compromise, and whites to give blacks more jobs. This view made him very popular with white politicians. His actions made him unpopular with other black leaders, such as W. E. B. Du Bois. Washington never publicly supported black political causes, but worked his entire life to help black individuals find the skills to be responsible for themselves.

The Quest for Equality

Booker T. Washington and black activist W.E.B. Du Bois had different ideas about how Blacks in the United States should pursue equality. Washington advised Blacks to accept their position in society. He thought Blacks should learn practical work skills and learn to be responsible for themselves. Du Bois said the fight for equality could not wait. He believed that talented black people should be able to attend college and become leaders.

In the chart below, list what you believe are the strong points of each man's argument. Then write a paragraph explaining which of the views is most valid. Use at least three sentences to support your answer.

Booker T. Washington   W.E.B. Du Bois

_____

_____

_____

_____

_____

Albert Schweitzer
Responsibility

Summary

Albert Schweitzer, a well-educated, world famous musician and theologian, gave up his career to become a physician. As an expression of his belief that people had a responsibility to help mankind, he established a hospital in Gabon, Africa, and devoted the remainder of his life to working in the hospital.

Concepts to Consider

Albert Schweitzer saw the need for organized charities, but he did not believe that they were the entire answer for helping people in need. He strongly believed that individuals should open their eyes to the needs of people around them. No effort to help, regardless of how small, would fail to have an impact. His belief in the need for individual response could be seen in the hospital he created. Patients were treated out-of-doors, in the midst of their own families, because Schweitzer knew that keeping them isolated in an unfamiliar place would add to their distress.

Schweitzer turned his life completely upside-down to follow his mission. He believed that all people would be happier if they looked for opportunities to help others in the same way.

Extended Responses

Discussion Topics

Objective: Students will compare Schweitzer's belief in personal responsibility for other people to the actions of organized charities.

- Make of list of organizations that help people in need. From what you know of these organizations, how is their work carried out (fund-raising drives, food and clothing banks)?

- Compare the work of these organizations to the work done by Albert Schweitzer.

Writing Activity—Page 22

Objective: Students will imagine what the effects might be of an act of concern between one person and another, leading them to understand that even small acts might have wide-ranging results.

Albert Schweitzer believed that every man had a "second job," that of caring for the needs of other people. No matter how busy a person is, he has the responsibility of working for the good of others, even with the smallest act. He told a story about a cab driver working in England during World War I. Not eligible for active duty, the driver devoted his time to helping soldiers find their way around London. He also provided safe transportation for them.

In the worksheet "You Can Help" students are asked to write a story that describes a sequence of events that might follow such an act.

Albert Schweitzer
Responsibility

Albert Schweitzer believed that all people should take personal responsibility for helping people. He called this responsibility "your second job." He once said that, "…what the world lacks most today is men who occupy themselves with the needs of other men."

Schweitzer was born on January 14, 1875, in Alsace, Germany (now France). He was educated in both France and Germany. Schweitzer studied science and music and he received an advanced degree in theology. He held posts at several universities. Before he was 30, he had won an international reputation as a writer on theology, and as Europe's premier organist and an authority on organ building.

In 1904, Schweitzer read an article in the Paris Missionary Society's publication, saying that there was an urgent need for physicians in Africa. Schweitzer, inspired by his feelings of responsibility, immediately enrolled as a medical assistant and completed his training. He went to the Paris Missionary Society to volunteer, but was turned down. They felt he was an "intellectual" who would undermine their missionary work with his ideas about religion.

Schweitzer could not give up his mission. He gave up all of his academic positions and cancelled all music engagements and contracts. So Schweitzer and his wife Helene began to raise the funds themselves. Their families did not approve of their plans, so they contacted friends for donations. Schweitzer went back to the Missionary Society with all of the funds needed to make the journey and to start a small hospital.

In 1913, Albert and his wife opened a hospital in Lambarene, Gabon. They began their work in a chicken coop. Over the years, Schweitzer built a large hospital and a medical station where thousands of Africans were treated yearly. At the outbreak of World War I, the Schweitzers were forced to return to Europe. Albert returned alone in 1924 to continue his missionary work. He was awarded the Nobel Peace Prize in 1953. The monetary award paid for improvements in his hospital facility.

Schweitzer stayed in Africa for the rest of his life. He retired as a surgeon, but continued to oversee the hospital until his death at the age of 90. His daughter Rhena continued his work for many years after his death. Albert and his wife Helene are both buried on the hospital grounds.

Albert Schweitzer gave up a promising career to devote himself to the care of other human beings. His efforts brought him worldwide fame, but it was more important to him that he had lived up to the responsibility he felt he had to the people of the world.

You Can Help

Every day you will see someone who needs help. Sometimes they need help with problems like a bully at school or a hard math lesson. Sometimes they are sad or have hurt feelings. There is always something you can do to help—even if you only say a kind word. Giving that help will make a difference

Think of a time when a friend needed help. Write a story that explains what was wrong and what you might have done to help. Finish your story by telling how that friend's day was different because you helped.

_____

_____

_____

_____

_____

_____

_____

_____

_____

_____

_____

_____

_____

_____

_____

_____

Abigail Adams
Loyalty

Summary

Abigail Adams, wife of President John Adams and mother of President John Quincy Adams, made her own contributions to the Revolutionary War. The political career of her husband forced the couple into long periods of separation, but Abigail's sense of loyalty to the emerging nation were more important than her personal happiness.

Concepts to Consider

Abigail Adams was not just an observer of the Revolutionary period; she participated in it. As an intelligent, well-read woman, she corresponded with her husband when he was away. Many of her ideas were ahead of their time. Abigail opposed slavery and believed in equal education for boys and girls. She believed that the political opinions of women were valuable, and should be considered by the makers of the new government.

She did not have a formal education, but read everything she could find: the Bible, history, sermons, philosophy, essays, and poetry. She became one of the most well-read women in America and one of the most influential women of her times.

Extended Responses

Discussion Topics

Objective: Students will examine Abigail Adams' support of her husband's political career.

• Abigail Adams felt that the best thing women could do for the Revolutionary cause was to support their husbands, freeing them to do the work that was necessary. Compose a list of ways that Abigail showed that support for her husband.

• What questions would you ask Abigail Adams in an interview about her life?

• What comparisons can you make between Abigail's role in the political world and women in politics today? How have things changed?

Writing Activity—Page 25

Objective: Students will use their knowledge about Abigail Adams to write a short essay about her loyalty.

The letters that Abigail Adams wrote to her husband tell us a lot about what her feelings were during a hard time in her life. In addition, they tell us a lot about the political circumstances of the Revolutionary period and about life in a Revolutionary household.

The worksheet "A Loyal Woman" asks the students to write a short essay expressing their ideas about Abigail Adams' life and her loyalty to her husband and her country.

Abigail Adams
Loyalty

Abigail Adams is probably best known as the wife of the second President of the United States, John Adams, and as mother of the sixth President, John Quincy Adams. But she was also a fierce patriot and a participant in the Revolutionary War.

Abigail Adams was born in Weymouth, Massachusetts, on November 11, 1744. She never went to school but was taught at home. In 1764, she married John Adams. Together they had five children. They made their home in Braintree, Massachusetts, where John was a lawyer and a circuit judge.

After ten years of happy married life, Abigail found her household broken up by the Revolutionary War. For the next ten years she had not only the care of the children on her hands, but also the farm to look after. Her husband was away from home much of that time, serving as a delegate to the Continental Congress, an elected officer under the Constitution, and as an envoy abroad. In 1784 she finally joined John Adams in Europe (where he was engaged in diplomatic missions), spending eight months in Paris and then three years in London. In 1788 the Adamses returned to the United States. During the 12 years of her husband's terms as Vice-President and President, Abigail divided her time between the capital and her home in Massachusetts.

Abigail Adams left a legacy of these times in her letters to her husband and family. Her letters show where she felt her loyalties were: with her husband and her country. As her husband's life became more dominated by politics, she willingly entered that world with him and gave him all the sympathy and advice she could muster. She felt that the best way for a woman of that time to show patriotism was to support the efforts of her husband and to free him to do the work that needed to be done. Her letters show that at times she was desperately lonely, yet she never asked or encouraged John to give up his political work.

Abigail shouldered a great deal of responsibility during her husband's career: she managed the farm and the family's finances singlehandedly and raised her children. She suffered the hearthside hardships of war: melting spoons to make bullets, weaving her own fabric for clothes. She housed soldiers in her own home. During Adams' career, she offered wise suggestions and advice to her husband, all of which he took very seriously. She helped Martha Washington with official entertaining, drawing on her experience of courts and society abroad, and continued the same entertaining as wife to President Adams.

After Adams' presidency, Abigail and John were able to be together again. They lived together until Abigail died in 1818. She is remembered as wife to one President and mother to a second, and as a voice and force of the American Revolution.

A Loyal Woman

Abigail Adams expressed her feelings in writing. Through her writings, we know about the work she had to do and the loneliness she felt when her husband was away. She also wrote about the importance of the patriot cause and shared her opinions about what was happening.

In the space below, write a paragraph about Abigail Adams and the way she showed her loyalty to her family and to her country. Write a second paragraph describing examples of loyal actions in your own family or community.

Robert E. Lee
Loyalty

Summary

Robert E. Lee, loyal to the United States and to his native state of Virginia, is forced to choose one over the other with the outbreak of the Civil War.

Concepts to Consider

There were many people who were affected by the Civil War in the same way that Robert E. Lee was affected. It was a war when family members fought against family members, and neighbors against neighbors.

However, Lee's experience was unique. After the war, he threw his heart into trying to restore the broken nation. His sense of loyalty to the United States did not disappear with the conflict, and he devoted himself to trying to reunite the nation.

Extended Responses

Discussion Topics

Objective: Students will examine episodes in Lee's life that illustrate his strong sense of loyalty.

• In a letter to his sister, Lee wrote, *"With all my devotion to the Union and the feeling of loyalty and duty of an American citizen, I have not been able to make up my mind to raise my hand against my relatives, my children, my home."* Theorize about what motives might have influenced Lee to stay in the Union Army instead of serving for the Confederacy.

• Explain the meaning of "Make your sons Americans." How does it relate to the beliefs of Robert E. Lee?

• Although it was not granted for 100 years (due to a mistake), Lee filed an application for a full pardon from the United States Government. Explain why this is significant.

Writing Activity—Page 28

Objective: Students will create a letter written to President Lincoln by Robert E. Lee that shows their understanding of the conflict he felt over his loyalties to nation and state.

Once Lee decided that he could not fight against his native state of Virginia, he had to resign from the United States Army as well as respond to President Lincoln's request that he lead the Union forces.

The worksheet "Dear Mr. President" asks the students to define the thoughts of Robert E. Lee as he resigns from the United States Army.

Robert E. Lee
Loyalty

Even as a cadet at West Point, Robert E. Lee was known for his upstanding personal character. Other cadets nicknamed him "The Marble Statue" because of his almost perfect record of behavior and academics.

Robert E. Lee was born near Montross, Virginia, on January 19, 1807. He was a serious boy, and spent many hours in his father's library. He grew up with a deep devotion to country life and to his native state of Virginia. That devotion continued his entire life. He entered the United States Military Academy in 1825, where classmates admired him for his intelligence, leadership qualities, and devotion to duty. He graduated with high honors in 1829 and began his career as a military engineer, supervising construction of a fort and flood control work. He gained notice and honors on the staff of Winfield Scott during the Mexican War.

The outbreak of the Civil War caused a serious dilemma for Robert E. Lee. Lee did not believe in slavery. He had freed the slaves he inherited from his family because he believed that slavery had an evil effect on masters as well as slaves. He hated the thought of a divided nation; he was not in favor of secession. But when Abraham Lincoln asked Lee to head the United States Army, Lee had to decide whether to fight for the nation he loved, or to stand by his native state. In the end he could not fight against Virginia. He retired from the U.S. Army.

Lee began the Civil War as military advisor to Confederate president, Jefferson Davis. In 1861, he became a full general and headed the Army of Northern Virginia. He successfully won many major battles in the war, including the Battles of the Seven Days and the Second Battle of Bull Run. But at Gettysburg in 1863, Lee lost to Union general George G. Meade, the turning point of the war. Lee's battered troops became tired and hungry, and in April 1865, they surrendered to General U.S. Grant, bringing the war to an end.

Robert E. Lee was loved by his troops and very much admired by military men in both the South and the North. After the war, he became the successful president of Washington College in Lexington, where he remained until he died in 1870. Lee was eager to see the hard feelings between the North and the South come to an end. He urged his friends and his students to accept the outcome of the war. He did all that he could to reduce the feelings of hatred and bitterness in the South. He applied for a complete pardon from the U.S. Government as an example to other Southerners. Although his sense of loyalty caused him to fight on the side of the Confederacy, the loyalty he always felt for his nation led him to urge Southerners to "Make your sons Americans."

Dear Mr. President

Once Lee decided that he could not fight against his native state of Virginia, he had to resign from the United States Army, as well as respond to President Lincoln's request that he lead the Union forces.

Imagine that you are Robert E. Lee. In the space below, write a letter to Abraham Lincoln, explaining your decision and the reasons behind it.

Mohandas Gandhi
Perseverance

Summary

Mohandas Gandhi, called *Mahatma* or "Great Soul" by the people of India, devoted his life to the betterment of his people, and to the cause of freeing India from British rule. He adopted a policy of nonviolent resistance, and despite hardship to himself, he persevered in following this policy.

Concepts to Consider

Mohandas Gandhi's method of nonviolent resistance is the basis of many civil rights movements, notably the work done by Martin Luther King, Jr. His philosophy became ingrained in his entire way of living, and despite arrests and other hardships, he persevered in following his beliefs.

Before reading the story, talk to students about various methods of nonviolent resistance: marches, sit-ins, petitions, fasts. Ask them about where they hear of these things occurring, and encourage discussion of how effective these methods seem to be.

Extended Responses

Discussion Topics

Objective: Students will examine methods of nonviolent resistance.

• One method used by Gandhi and by people today is a boycott. Using a dictionary, define the word "boycott." Rephrase the definition in a way that would help you explain it to a younger student.

• How do boycotts influence leaders? Imagine that the maker of your favorite candy bar is using packaging that is wasteful and that you want them to change it. Make an outline of the steps you would take and how the manufacturer might respond.

Writing Activity—Page 31

Objective: Students will apply Gandhi's philosophy to situations that might occur in their own lives.

Gandhi developed a method of direct social action, based upon principles of courage, nonviolence, and truth, which he called *Satsygraha*. In this method, the way people behave is more important than what they achieve.

The worksheet "Satsygraha" asks students to examine situations and describe how Gandhi might respond.

Mohandas Gandhi
Perseverance

Mohandas Gandhi was an important spiritual and political leader in India. He helped free India from British control by a unique method of nonviolent resistance, and is honored by the people of India as the father of their nation.

Gandhi was born on October 2, 1869, in Porbandar, India. His parents belonged to the vaisya (merchant) caste of Hindus. His parents arranged a marriage for him, which took place when Gandhi was 13 years old. At the age of 19, Gandhi left his wife and son in India to study law in London. He returned to India but did not succeed in establishing a law practice.

In 1893, Gandhi went to do some legal work in South Africa, then under British control. Almost immediately he was abused because he was an Indian who claimed his rights as a British subject. He saw that all Indians suffered from discrimination. He stayed in South Africa for 21 years to work for Indian rights.

Gandhi led many campaigns for Indian rights in South Africa. He developed a method of nonviolent direct social action that he called *Satyagraha*. Gandhi believed that the way people behaved was more important than what they finally achieved. His goal was to draw attention to racial discrimination both by the oppressors and the oppressed. He felt that if both sides recognized the inequalities, they would eventually work together to end it. Gandhi promoted campaigns of civil disobedience and organized a strike among Indian miners. He was arrested many times by the British, but his efforts brought many reforms.

Gandhi returned to India in 1915, and within five years had become the leader of the Indian nationalist movement. In 1919, the British tried to pass two bills that would make it illegal to organize any opposition to the government. Gandhi led a campaign that prevented the passage of one of the bills. The other bill was never enforced. When riots broke out, Gandhi called off the campaign. He then fasted to impress people with the need to be nonviolent. In 1930, the British passed the Salt Act, which made it a crime to own salt not bought from the government. To protest, Gandhi led a group of hundreds of people on a 200-mile march to the sea where they made their own salt.

Gandhi continued his work for Indian independence through 1947, when Great Britain granted freedom to India. He was arrested and jailed many times. He did not believe there was any shame in being jailed for a good cause. For the remainder of his life, Gandhi worked to unite the Muslims and the Hindus. In January, 1948, he started a fast in order to encourage the leaders of the two groups to stop fighting. After five days, they agreed and his fast ended. Twelve days later, Gandhi was killed by a Hindu who opposed Gandhi's beliefs. As Gandhi died, he spoke words of forgiveness for his assassin.

Satsygraha

Mohandas Gandhi's philosophy of *Satsygraha* is based on the belief that the way people behave is more important that what they ultimately achieve. Look at the situations described below. Using Gandhi's philosophy, decide what the best behavior would be in each situation. Explain why you think it is the best thing to do.

An old house in your neighborhood has been empty for a long time. Your friends think it's fun to break the windows in the old house.	Two kindergarten kids are having a fist fight on the sidewalk after school. It's really funny to watch, and there are no adults nearby.
Your teacher assigns a book to read for a book report. You've already read the book, and wonder if you can do a report without reading it again.	Your parents are going out and will be back by 11:00. They expect you to stay home. Your friend asks you to see a movie that ends at 10:00.

Albert Einstein

Perseverance

Summary

Before he became recognized as a brilliant scientist, Albert Einstein struggled with failures in school and difficulties in finding a career.

Concepts to Consider

It takes a special kind of perseverance to withstand the frustrations and disappointments that can come with failures in school and in a career. A person who overcomes such difficulties must persevere by believing in himself and his goals. Albert Einstein had that kind of perseverance.

He often told a story about receiving a "wonder" at about age five: a compass. His fascination with the magnetic needle in that compass opened a door for him to the sense that there had to be "something behind things, something deeply hidden." That sense kept him working and studying the things that he truly enjoyed, despite stifling school situations and a career outside his course of study. That inner drive to figure out how the world worked drove Einstein toward his revolutionary studies.

Extended Responses

Discussion Topics

Objective: Students will summarize the obstacles that Einstein faced. They will then identify a goal of their own and speculate about what might make that goal difficult to attain.

• Although Einstein did not have a troubled life, he did have a problem in finding out what he really wanted to achieve. Make a list of things that might have caused this problem.

• Select a goal that you have set in your own life. Design a plan that will help you reach that goal. Now try to predict what circumstances might keep you from reaching your goal.

Writing Activity—Page 34

Objective: Students will make an acrostic chart of statements relating to perseverance.

Albert Einstein found his life's work after many years of moving from one thing to another. For many reasons, this is true of many people. The frustration of looking for what one wants in life can undermine a person's happiness and success.

The worksheet "Perseverance" asks students to create an acrostic chart made up of sentences they have written to encourage perseverance.

Albert Einstein
Perseverance

There was little in the early life of Albert Einstein to indicate that he would become one of the greatest scientists of all time. When he was a young child, his parents had fears that he might be somewhat backward. He did not do especially well in school. One of his teachers even suggested that Albert leave school because his presence was so disrupting to the rest of the students.

There were some indications of Einstein's true capabilities. Family legend says he was a slow talker because he thought carefully about what he was going to say. He had the perseverance to build houses of cards that were many stories high.

Albert Einstein was born in Germany on March 14, 1879. His father was a manufacturer of electrical parts. Business failure forced the family to move first to Munich and later to Milan, Italy. Albert attended school, but he disliked the system of rigid discipline, and learned more studying mathematics, philosophy, and science at home. At age fifteen, he quit high school to join his parents in Italy. He took an entrance examination for the Swiss Federal Institute of Technology in 1895, but failed. He managed to graduate from a school in Aarau, Switzerland, in 1900. He moved to the University of Zurich and started his study of physics.

After Einstein graduated with an undistinguished record, he made a number of efforts to get a university job, but failed. He found occasional jobs as a tutor or a substitute teacher. He felt he was a burden to his family, and wondered if he had been mistaken in trying to become a physicist. Finally he got a position at the Swiss Patent Office in Bern. The regular salary and the stimulating work evaluating patent claims freed Einstein. He now had time to devote his thoughts to physics, his true interest.

In 1905, Einstein submitted three papers to a German scientific journal. Each paper became the basis of a new branch of physics: quantum mechanics, the relativity of time, and Brownian motion. The papers gained him immediate attention. He became a professor of theoretical sciences at the University of Zurich, then moved on to the University of Prague and various other universities. He continued to study and publish his revolutionary theories. In 1933 he moved to the United States to join the Institute for Advanced Study in Princeton, New Jersey. He took part in atomic research in the United States, and was instrumental in advising the government about the possibilities of the atomic bomb.

Albert Einstein was always vitally interested in human affairs. He was a strong supporter of a world government, which he felt would be necessary to keep peace in an atomic world. The difficulties he faced as a child and young man trying to get an education and establish a career taught him to believe that the best education was obtained when people were free to follow their own interests.

Perseverance Chart

Sometimes it can be very hard to keep going, or persevere, when you have a proble
Use a dictionary to find the definition of "Perseverance." Create a "Perseverance Chart
to remind and encourage yourself to keep trying. Use each letter in the word
perseverance to start a sentence that either describes what perseverance is, or that will
encourage you to persevere.

P _____

E _____

R _____

S _____

E _____

V _____

E _____

R _____

A _____

N _____

C _____

E _____

Sitting Bull
Honesty

Summary

A legendary Native American warrior and leader, Sitting Bull was also honest, courageous, and trustworthy. In his struggle to hold on to his people's land, he did not lose sight of his responsibility for caring for them. He dealt honestly with the U.S government, never breaking a treaty or attacking a white settlement.

Concepts to Consider

A person's behavior is judged on the basis of the culture's standards. As a whole, Sitting Bull is famous for leading the Sioux against the U.S. government. He was also thought to be responsible for Custer's defeat at the Little Big Horn.

Looking at contemporary accounts, it is apparent that there was a lot of good, honest, honorable behavior in Sitting Bull's life. It is widely accepted that his actions were driven by concern for his people and their future, not personal gain or a desire for revenge.

Extended Responses

Discussion Topics

Objective: Students will examine issues that arose as settlers moved into Native American lands. They will propose solutions that might have avoided the conflicts.

- When gold was discovered in the Black Hills, the government wanted the land open for the prospectors. The Sioux had been promised that land for their own. Prepare a list of points to support each side of the argument.

- How would you prioritize these points based on the rights of Native Americans versus prospectors?

- Propose a solution to the conflict.

Writing Activity—Page 36

Objective: Students will write definitions for character traits related to honesty. They will also draw conclusions about how each of the words relates to honesty.

Honesty relates to many other character traits. Honest behavior exhibits itself in many different ways.

The worksheet "Honesty Is…" asks students to define words that are related to the trait of honesty. They are also asked to draw their own conclusions about how each trait relates to honest behavior.

Sitting Bull
Honesty

Sitting Bull was a famous medicine man and leader of the Hunkpapa Sioux. Many people think that he was the leader of the Native Americans at the battle of the Little Bighorn, in which Lieutenant Colonel George Custer died. In fact, he acted as the main medicine man in preparation for the confrontation.

Sitting Bull was born around 1831, in what is now South Dakota. His father gave him his name when he showed great bravery in a fight. As he grew older, he developed a reputation among his own people as being generous, wise, honest, sincere, and devoted to his family and his people. He was a natural leader, and gained respect both among the Native Americans and among the white people. Sitting Bull was generous and friendly to the white settlers around him.

As settlers moved across the land, Sioux territory was taken away. Sitting Bull became a member of the Strong Heart society, who tried to gain back some of the lost hunting land. However, the U.S. Army kept moving into this land, causing economic problems for the tribes. From 1863 to 1868 the Sioux fought the army's advance. Around 1867, Sitting Bull became the principal chief of the entire Sioux nation. A short time later, the Fort Laramie treaty was signed by other Sioux leaders and the U.S. Government. The treaty promised the Black Hills would remain in Sioux possession forever.

In the 1870s, gold was found in the Black Hills, bringing thousands of miners into the area. The government ordered the Sioux onto reservations. The Native Americans ignored the order, and on June 17, 1876, the Sioux, Cheyenne, and Arapaho joined forces to stop the army at the Battle of the Rosebud. On June 25, George Armstrong Custer led 200 men into the Native village along the Little Big Horn River. By the end of the day, Custer and his army were dead.

The army continued to chase the Natives, and Sitting Bull took his tribe to Canada for safety. They lived there in peace until a shortage of buffalo sent them back to the United States. Sitting Bull was arrested and his people were sent to reservations. Sitting Bull sat in prison for two years before he rejoined his tribe.

Sitting Bull never broke a treaty with the U.S. Government. Treaties were broken by the white settlers when they decided they wanted Native American land. More than one army officer formed a trusting relationship with him and none of them were disappointed. Sitting Bull also kept his promises to his people—to lead them with courage and to protect them and their way of life.

Sitting Bull traveled with Buffalo Bill's Wild West Show for a few months to earn money. He returned to the reservation, and was arrested again in 1890 for participating in a new religion called the Ghost Dance. When tribe members tried to rescue him on December 15, 1890, he was shot and killed.

Just Like Honest

If you look in a thesaurus, you will see many words that mean the same thing or are similar to the word "honest." It is important to recognize that honesty is the basis for a lot of good character traits.

Look at the words below. Write the definition for each of the words. Under each definition, explain how that word is the same as or is related to the word "honest."

Trustworthy	**Just**
Definition:	Definition:
How does it relate to "Honesty"?	How does it relate to "Honesty"?
Conscientious	**Honorable**
Definition:	Definition:
How does it relate to "Honesty"?	How does it relate to "Honesty"?
Sincere	**Incorruptible**
Definition:	Definition:
How does it relate to "Honesty"?	How does it relate to "Honesty"?

George Washington
Honesty

Summary

Leaders in the Revolutionary era chose George Washington to lead the army and then to lead the country because of his reputation for honesty and loyalty. In many ways he has become a symbol for perfect leadership.

Concepts to Consider

George Washington has become such a legendary figure that many students don't become familiar with the man as a whole. The story about Washington chopping down the cherry tree is an example of how this happens. There were many aspects of Washington's character that made him a great leader.

It is valuable for students to look at legends that are familiar to them: Abraham Lincoln, Paul Bunyan, Johnny Appleseed, Daniel Boone, Pocahontas. Evaluating what it is that makes each of these people legendary is a good way to see how good character makes good leaders.

Extended Responses

Discussion Topics

Objective: Students will name individuals, real or fictional, that have come to symbolize good character traits.

- George Washington and Abraham Lincoln (Honest Abe) are two Presidents that have become legendary. Make a list of other people, real or fictional, who have become legends because of their character traits.

- Select one of these people and explain what about them has made them legendary.

- Evaluate the significance of legendary figures.

Writing Activity—Page 40

Objective: Students will tell why they think honesty is an important quality in a leader. They will select other character traits that they feel are part of good leadership and explain why they chose them.

The quality of leadership chosen by the early Americans was crucial to the survival of the emerging nation. Fortunately, Washington and the other leaders of the new nation realized that they must act cautiously because they were setting precedents for the leaders of the future.

The worksheet "Honesty in Leadership" asks students to explain why they think it is necessary for a leader of a nation or of any group to be honest. They are then asked to select other character traits that they feel are important to good leadership and explain why those traits were chosen.

George Washington
Honesty

George Washington probably did not chop down a cherry tree, then confess to his father, saying, "I cannot tell a lie." But this story and others like it show that people were willing to believe anything about Washington's honesty.

George Washington was born in 1732 into the family of a wealthy Virginia planter. He only went to school until he was about age 15. Washington had two main interests: military arts and western expansion. At 16 he helped survey land for Thomas, Lord Fairfax. He was commissioned a lieutenant colonel in the army in 1754, and fought the first skirmishes of what grew into the French and Indian War. The next year, as an aide to General Edward Braddock, he escaped injury although four bullets ripped his coat and two horses were shot from under him.

From 1759 to the outbreak of the American Revolution, Washington managed the land around his home, Mount Vernon, and served in the Virginia House of Burgesses. He married a widow, Martha Custis, and devoted himself to a busy and happy life. But like his fellow planters, Washington felt himself exploited by British merchants and hampered by British laws. As the quarrel with Britain became more serious, he firmly voiced his resistance to British restrictions.

When the Second Continental Congress assembled in Philadelphia in May 1775, Washington was elected Commander in Chief of the Continental Army. On July 3, 1775, at Cambridge, Massachusetts, he took command of his ill-trained troops and started into a war that was to last six long years.

Washington was beloved by his men. At the end of the war, Congress had very little money. There were rumors that they were planning to disband the army without paying the men. The soldiers were ready to march on Congress. Washington called his officers together and asked them to be patient. He gave them his promise that he would do everything in his power to see that they were treated fairly. They believed in Washington's honesty; they waited, and were paid.

After the war, Washington was instrumental in building the new government. When the new Constitution was ratified, he was elected President. He served two terms. He was cautious and thoughtful in the way he led the country. He felt that he was setting a precedent. How he acted as President would influence the actions of presidents to follow him.

Washington refused a third term as President and retired to Mount Vernon with Martha. But his advice and help were needed by the new government up until the time of his death. Washington died on December 14, 1799. Thousands of American people wore black mourning clothes for months. His reputation as a strong, honest leader made him beloved and respected throughout the world.

Honest Leadership

Because George Washington had a reputation for being honest, Americans trusted him to be the first President of the United States. Other leaders in the Revolutionary Period trusted Washington to lead the nation while they were working out the details of how the new government would work.

Do you think that it is important for leaders today to be honest? Write your answer the space below. Support your answer with at least three reasons.

John Muir
Respect

Summary

John Muir was a farmer, inventor, sheepherder, naturalist, explorer, writer, and conservationist. He is best known for his exploration of the Yosemite Valley and his efforts to convince the national government to preserve large areas of natural land for future generations.

Concepts to Consider

Significant as it is today, conservation was not a well-known concept during John Muir's lifetime. People looked at the world around them with an eye to how it could be used to benefit them. John Muir's contribution was to encourage respect for the natural world.

In addition to the biography, provide pictures or photographs of the Yosemite Valley or other areas visited by John Muir to give students a sense of the grandeur he hoped to save. Many students may have visited these areas and will have information to share.

Extended Responses

Discussion Topics

Objective: Students will discuss their own experiences in the outdoors. They will also discover ways in which they can contribute to conservation of natural resources.

• Create a list of National Parks. Poll the class to see how many students have visited a National Park. Ask individuals to share their stories.

• John Muir said that nature was like a factory: the workers, the machines, and the different departments were all interconnected. He saw the connection between rocks, soil, plants, water, and animals—including humans. How would you restate that belief?

• Identify conservation efforts that are taking place in the world today. Brainstorm a list of ways that students can help these efforts.

Writing Activity—Page 43

Objective: Students will explain why preserving parts of the wilderness is important to future generations.

John Muir is often called the father of the United States' National Park system. When he saw areas of spectacular beauty, he wanted those sights saved for future generations. He spent a lot of his life speaking and writing articles and letters in an effort to save these areas.

The worksheet "Save Our Land" asks students to write a letter to the President or other government official, asking for the protection of a wildlife area that is special to them.

John Muir
Respect

In 1868, John Muir made his first visit to the Yosemite Valley in California. His visit would change the world.

Muir was born in Dunbar, Scotland, moving to Wisconsin when he was 11 years old. There he helped his father with the family farm, clearing the forest, plowing, and digging wells. John's father was a harsh parent, and worked his family from dawn to dark. Whenever he was allowed away from his work, John would roam the fields and woods around the farm. He grew to love and respect the natural world.

John did not have much schooling, but he loved to read and study. He was a natural inventor. His inventions included an alarm clock that tipped the sleeping person out of bed. Friends convinced him to take his inventions to the state fair where he won prizes for them. People who noticed his talents helped him enter the University of Wisconsin, where he studied for three years.

Over the next few years, Muir worked as a mechanic, taking long hikes into the wilderness in his free time. In 1867, an accident caused him to lose the sight in one eye. The other eye also failed, and although he eventually recovered, he never again took for granted the things that were so important for him to see: the wonders of nature.

Muir's first wilderness adventure was a thousand-mile walk from Kentucky to Georgia. He hoped to travel on to the Amazon River but caught malaria in Florida. Instead of South America, he headed for California. When he asked where he should go to see something wild, he was sent to the Yosemite Valley.

John Muir was to return to Yosemite again and again. At first he worked there as a shepherd and in a sawmill, but as he grew to appreciate the Yosemite Valley's beauty, he began to realize that the natural surroundings had to be protected. Vast areas of the Sierra Nevada Mountains were being destroyed for livestock and lumber. He began to see the natural world as one living organism, each part depending on the others for life and survival. He believed that every part of nature was important for itself, not just for what it provided for human beings.

Muir visited other wildlands in the world: other parts of California, Utah, Nevada, and Alaska. Yosemite was always his favorite. He served as a guide to the Yosemite Valley to many important people of his day, including Ralph Waldo Emerson and Theodore Roosevelt. The letters and articles he wrote were instrumental in convincing the United States government to set aside large areas of forested land for preservation. In his own words, Muir wanted generations to come to enjoy the nation's natural beauty, and to "do something for the wilderness and make the mountains glad."

Save Our Land

What natural area is especially important to you? Why is it important? Write a letter to the President asking him to help preserve this place for future generations. Include some comments that explain why people should respect nature.

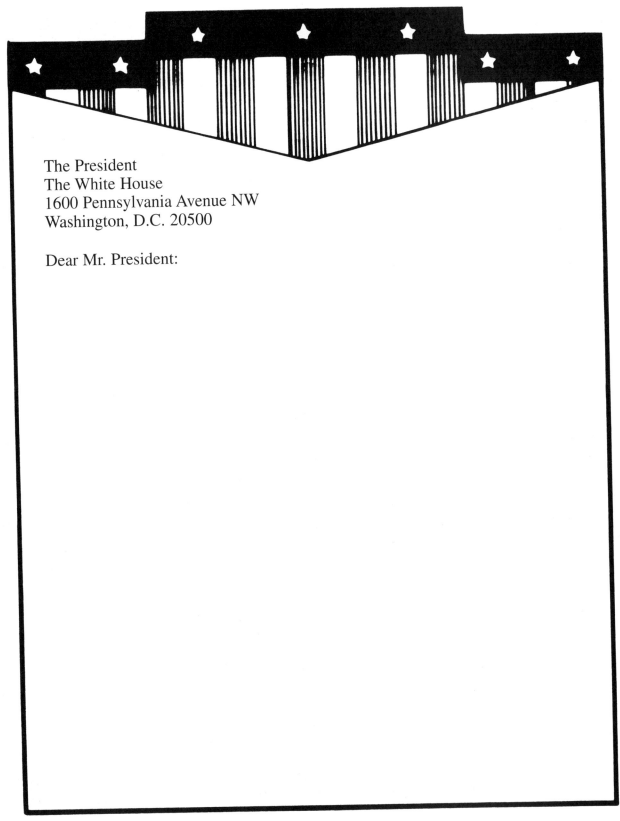

The President
The White House
1600 Pennsylvania Avenue NW
Washington, D.C. 20500

Dear Mr. President:

Martin Luther King, Jr.
Respect

Summary

Dr. Martin Luther King, Jr., broke many laws in carrying through his efforts to end segregation, but still insisted that it was important to maintain respect for the law.

Concepts to Consider

Because the work of civil rights workers has been highly respected, it may not occur to students that many of the things they did were against the law. The definition of civil disobedience expresses it clearly—refusing to obey unjust laws in order to try to change them.

After reading the biography, talk to the students to find out how much they know about civil rights movements in the United States and in other places of the world. Discuss various aspects of civil disobedience to help them understand the conflicts and events that took place. Examples: sit-ins, boycotts, passive resistance, civil rights, Jim Crow laws, segregation/desegregation, Freedom Riders.

Extended Responses

Discussion Topics

Objective: Students will understand the realities of racial discrimination and examine Dr. Martin Luther King, Jr.'s feelings about the law.

• Define the phrase "civil disobedience." How does this compare with Dr. King's ideas about obeying the law?

• Compare and contrast the way Blacks were treated in the 1950s and 1960s to the way they are treated today. Have things improved? Are there still changes to be made?

• Make a list of groups of people who are affected by discrimination now.

Writing Activity—Page 46

Objective: Students will understand that discrimination is a way of showing a lack of respect. They will give examples of how they can show respect for other people.

Segregation or any kind of discriminatory behavior is an expression of a lack of respect for other individuals. Civil rights workers were not fighting just to gain specific rights, but to command respect for themselves as human beings.

In the worksheet "Respect for Other People," students will be asked to give examples of how they, as individuals, can show respect for all people.

Martin Luther King, Jr.
Respect

Dr. Martin Luther King, Jr. was born on January 15, 1929 in Atlanta, Georgia. King was a Baptist minister who became one of the most important leaders of the civil rights movement in the United States. He believed in using non-violent means to achieve civil rights reform.

Martin Luther King, Jr. grew up in a time when society in parts of the United States was segregated. In some places, Blacks went to separate schools, and were not allowed in some hotels and restaurants. They were not allowed to vote. Blacks were sometimes paid less than whites because of their race. They had to sit in the back of public buses. Martin hated being treated unfairly. He wanted to change the system, so he decided to become a minister like his father. As a church leader, he could speak out against inequality.

In 1955, Rosa Parks, a black woman, was arrested for refusing to give up her seat on a bus to a white man. Dr. King helped organize a bus boycott. During the boycott his house was bombed. He told his followers not to answer violence with violence. "We must meet hate with love," he said. He believed that the struggle for equality had to be based on passive resistance, not violent confrontation.

Dr. King spent many years lecturing around the country and organizing demonstrations, boycotts, and marches. Sometimes he was arrested for his actions. He joined sit-ins where black people sat at "white only" lunch counters and waiting rooms to protest unfair segregation laws. He organized a voter registration drive in Selma, Alabama, then led 30,000 marchers to the state capital.

There were many people in the United States that did not agree with King's views. People did not understand why King was willing to break the law in order to demonstrate. In a letter written while he was in jail, King explained that he had great respect for the law. He did not believe in breaking laws that were fair or just. If a law was intended to keep a certain group of people from enjoying the rights shared by everyone else, it was not just. In that case, King felt that people had a responsibility to not obey the law. If people broke a law, even an unjust one, they should "do so openly, lovingly, and with a willingness to accept the penalty."

In 1963, Dr. King spoke to a gathering of 200,000 people, black and white, in Washington, D.C. He made a stirring speech which is known as the "I Have A Dream" speech. In the speech he said, "I have a dream that my four little children will one day live in a nation where they will not be judged by the color of their skin but by the content of their character."

In 1968, Dr. King was shot and killed on a motel balcony in Memphis, Tennessee. The whole world mourned his death.

Respect for Other People

When civil rights workers fought to end segregation, they had very specific complaints about how Blacks were treated. Segregation was allowed to exist because one group of people did not respect another group. They did not respect their rights, nor did they respect them as individuals.

Think of five ways that you can show respect for other people. Write your answers in the hearts below.

1.

2.

3.

4.

5.

Sacagawea
Trustworthiness

Summary

A Shoshone woman named Sacagawea made significant contributions to the success of the Lewis and Clark expedition. She proved herself to be trustworthy in her dealings with her native tribe and with the explorers.

Concepts to Consider

Sacagawea found herself in a position where her actions could be seen as disloyal to both groups of people she was dealing with: the explorers who needed the help of the Shoshone, and her native people who had no reason to trust the white intruders. Both groups trusted her to help them settle the disagreement because she had already proven herself trustworthy.

Poll the students about times when they have been called upon to be trustworthy. Discuss how they have shown their trustworthiness in the past, and how the effects of not being trustworthy might change their lives. Has being trustworthy ever interfered with their own plans and desires?

Extended Responses

Discussion Topics

Objective: Students will question the reasons that Sacagawea remained trustworthy to the Lewis and Clark expedition, in spite of the possible impacts on her own people.

• Do you agree with Sacagawea's efforts in helping Lewis and Clark? Why or why not?

• What motives do you think Sacagawea might have had in telling Lewis and Clark about the Shoshone's plans?

• Were Sacagawea's actions harmful or beneficial to the Shoshone? Explain your answer.

Writing Activity—Page 49

Objective: Students will decide what constitutes trustworthy behavior in several situations.

A person is trustworthy when they show other people that they can be relied upon to keep promises and to follow through on what they are asked to do or have said they will do.

The worksheet "Worthy of Trust" asks students to evaluate six situations and determine what action they would take to be trustworthy.

Sacagawea
Trustworthiness

Sacagawea was a member of the Lewis and Clark expedition to the Pacific Ocean in 1804 and 1805. They asked her to join their group to act as interpreter with the Shoshone tribe, but Sacagawea played a much more important role in the expedition.

Sacagawea's name means *Bird Woman*. She was born among the Shoshone, or Snake, tribe of Idaho sometime around 1787. When she was 11, an enemy tribe captured her and sold her as a slave to a French-Canadian trader, Toussaint Charbonneau. Lewis and Clark met Charbonneau and Sacagawea when their expedition passed through the Fort Mandan Trading Post on the Missouri River. Charbonneau could speak Sioux and French. The explorers asked Charbonneau to bring Sacagawea and her newborn baby because she spoke Shoshone.

Although at first the white explorers had little respect or concern for Sacagawea, over time their feelings changed. Having more knowledge of plants and animals, she was instrumental in helping the party find food along the trail. When the group's boats overturned, it was Sacagawea who kept a clear head and saved most of their food and supplies from the rapidly-moving river. When they reached the Continental Divide, Clark was forced to choose which trail they would take over the mountains. Sacagawea knew the area and led them to a trail that proved to be the best one they could have taken.

While crossing the Divide, the group met relatives of Sacagawea among the Shoshone. Lewis and Clark needed the help of the Shoshone to complete their mission. The Shoshone would be able to sell them horses and food that they would need to finish their journey to the Pacific Ocean and back. The Shoshone had never seen white men. The exploration party feared that Sacagawea might leave them to rejoin her tribe.

Sacagawea did miss her people. Meeting with her family members made her want to return to the Shoshone, but Lewis and Clark had treated her with more respect than she had ever received before. They showed their respect in many ways: caring for her while she was sick, and giving her a horse so that she and her baby could ride. While with the Shoshone, she heard tribe members saying that they had lied to Lewis and Clark. They were not planning to give them horses and intended to desert the party. Sacagawea went to Lewis and Clark and told them. With her help, they persuaded the Shoshone to sell them horses in exchange for guns. Both sides trusted Sacagawea not to betray them.

Not much is known about Sacagawea after she returned. She probably died around 1812 in South Dakota. Her role in the explorations of Lewis and Clark and to the expansion of the United States was not recognized for many years.

Worthy of Trust

You become trustworthy when you act in a way that shows people you can be trusted follow through on your word and to make responsible decisions. Read the situations elow. Under each, write a short paragraph telling what trustworthy behavior would be each case. Explain why the action you've chosen shows trustworthiness.

Your mom told you to come home right after school, but your friends want to play at the park. Your mom's at work and won't be home for three more hours. What should you do?	You're spending the afternoon at your friend's house. You decide to go visit another friend. Should you let your mom know?
Your neighbor hired you to water his plants while he's away for two weeks. Your friend's family invited you to go on an overnight trip with them. What should you do?	You're at your friend's house, upstairs in his room. Your friend takes some pills out of his drawer and starts to talk to you about how fun it is to take them. What should you do?

Biographies That Build Character   © EDUPRESS, INC.   EP343

Abraham Lincoln

Trustworthiness

Summary

Abraham Lincoln was trustworthy in nearly every aspect of his life. People trusted him enough to elect him President at a crucial time in American history.

Concepts to Consider

Like George Washington, Abraham Lincoln's reputation is almost larger than life. Students are probably familiar with legends about Lincoln studying before the fireplace, walking 20 miles to return a book, splitting logs to make rails. There is truth in all of these legends.

Lincoln was a man with a complex personality. His character cannot be defined by one trait. All of the positive traits he possessed made him an important, influential man, capable of great leadership in a time of immense trouble.

Extended Responses

Discussion Topics

Objective: Students will discuss what they already know about Abraham Lincoln and make an evaluation about his character.

- Recall some stories you have heard or read about Abraham Lincoln. For each story, decide what character trait is presented.

- Do you think these legends are true? Explain why or why not.

- If you had to select one character trait to describe Lincoln, what would it be? Support your answer.

Writing Activity—Page 52

Objective: Students will find a set of words that are similar in meaning to the word trustworthy. They will then use those words to create a word-search puzzle to be solved by another student.

When you describe a trustworthy person, many additional character traits come to mind. Recognizing words that are related to or similar to "trustworthy" will help students understand the relationship between trustworthiness and other character traits.

The worksheet "Trustworthy" asks students to create a list of words similar in meaning or related to "trustworthy." They are then asked to use the words to create a word search puzzle for another student to solve.

Abraham Lincoln
Trustworthiness

Abraham Lincoln did many things in his lifetime: storekeeper, surveyor, lawyer, politician, and President of the United States. Although he was not always financially successful, he was always well-liked, respected, and trusted.

Lincoln was born on February 12, 1809, in Kentucky. His father was a farmer. In 1816, the family moved to Indiana. Abe helped his father clear trees from the land and build a new cabin. In 1818, Abe's mother Nancy died, leaving her husband, son, and daughter alone.

Lincoln had less than a full year of real schooling. But he loved to read, and studied as much as he could to educate himself. He often borrowed books, and could be relied upon to always return them. A history of the U.S. and a biography of George Washington were among the few books he owned. Lincoln's first profession after leaving home was storekeeper. He went into partnership with another man in purchasing a store. They were not able to make the store successful and eventually had to close the business. Lincoln's partner left Abe with money owed on the business. With hard work, Lincoln paid the debts.

Friends recommended that Abe read law, which was the usual way of becoming a lawyer at that time. He read and studied law books, and began his law practice in New Salem, Illinois. In 1842, he married Mary Todd, and the two settled down to raise a family in Springfield, Illinois. Lincoln was a successful lawyer and had a reputation for being unfailingly honest. He also became active in politics at this time. He served in the Illinois state legislature.

Lincoln gained national attention when he participated in a series of debates with Stephen Douglas in 1858. Both men were running for the U.S. Senate. The debates were about the extension of slavery into free territory. Lincoln believed that slavery was evil and would someday have to end. But he also believed new states had the right to make the decision for or against slavery for themselves.

Lincoln was elected President in 1860. He belonged to the new, antislavery Republican Party. The slave-holding states were angry at his election, causing them to withdraw from the Union and form their own government. Lincoln knew that in order for the country to survive, the states had to stay together. Only six weeks after Lincoln became President, the Civil War began. Lincoln proved to be a strong, intelligent leader. His army and his military leaders trusted his leadership, even through the worst parts of the War. In 1863, he issued the Emancipation Proclamation, freeing the slaves. The war ended in 1865.

Lincoln's dream was to bring the South peacefully back into the Union and rebuild the nation. His determination to keep working, breaking no trust with any person on his way, led him to almost seeing his dream complete. Lincoln was assassinated on April 14, 1865, just five days after the Civil War ended, but his reputation for being honest and trustworthy has never died.

Trustworthy

There are many words that are similar in meaning to "trustworthy". Use a thesaurus to make a list. Use the words to make a word-search puzzle. Then trade with a classmate and solve each other's puzzles.

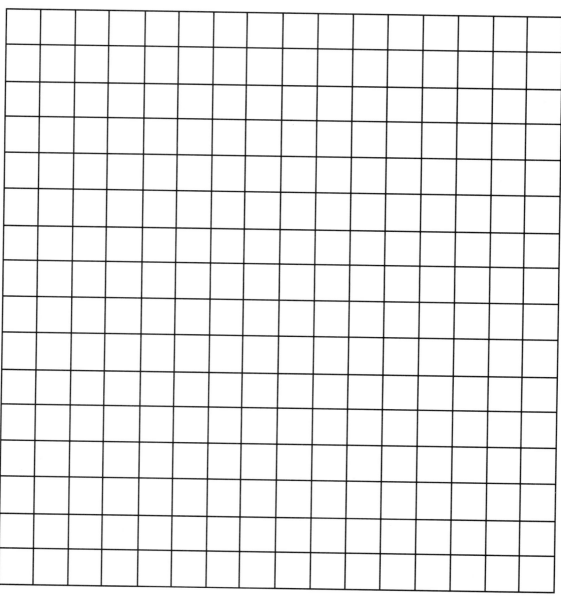

Word List:

Cesar Chavez
Fairness

Summary

Cesar Chavez, whose family lost their farm and became migrant workers, created an organization to help workers secure fair treatment and better working conditions.

Concepts to Consider

Cesar Chavez devoted his life to helping farm workers gain fair treatment from the system they worked for. The workers were not asking for equality, just for working conditions that would give them a more stable way of life.

After reading the biography, discuss the working conditions of these people with your students. Explain the use of peaceful strikes and boycotts. Help students to define these words.

Extended Responses

Discussion Topics

Objective: Students will discuss the issues that Cesar Chavez was working to improve and will make a judgment about whether or not his demands were fair.

- What conclusions can you reach about the effects of migrant living on adults? What about the effects on the children?

- One way Chavez fought for change was to stage a boycott. Define the term. How do you think a boycott would lead to change?

- Do you think that the demands made by the farm workers were fair? Support your answer.

Writing Activity—Page 55

Objective: Students will understand the purpose and use of a petition. They will understand the demands of the farm workers well enough to list some of the grievances in the form of a petition.

A petition is a useful way to organize the thoughts of a group in order to present their position to other people.

The worksheet "Petition to Farmers" asks the students to list some of the grievances of the farm workers and to explain their understanding of why each grievance should be listed.

53

Cesar Chavez
Fairness

Cesar Estrada Chavez was born March 31, 1927, near Yuma, Arizona. His grandfather owned a ranch. Chavez' father worked on the family ranch and owned a store in the Gila Valley. His family lived in an apartment above the store.

Chavez began school at age 7, but he found it hard because his family spoke only Spanish. Chavez preferred to learn from his uncles and grandparents, who read to him in Spanish. In addition, Chavez learned from his mother. She believed violence and selfishness were wrong, and she taught these lessons to her children.

In the 1930s, Chavez' father lost his business in the Great Depression and the family moved back to the ranch. A severe drought forced the family to give up the ranch. Chavez and his family packed their belongings and headed to California. They became part of the migrant farm worker community, traveling from farm to farm to pick fruits and vegetables during harvest seasons.

Migrant workers faced terrible living and working conditions. They lived in overcrowded migrant camps and were often forced to sleep in their cars. They were paid small wages for many hours of work, sometimes only a few cents a day. On many ranches there were no toilets in the fields. Although farmers provided water, they often charged the workers for the water and forced them to share rusty metal cups. The workers were exposed to pesticides that the farmers used to protect their crops. Migrant children could only attend school for short periods of time, and teachers often gave them little attention.

Once Chavez completed the eighth grade, he quit school and worked full time in the fields. His family was able to rent a small cottage in San Jose and make it their home. In 1944, Chavez joined the navy and served in World War II. He returned to California and married, moving into a one-room shack. Chavez again worked in the fields, but he began to fight for change. In 1948, he took part in his first strike in protest of low wages and poor working conditions. Over the next 40 years Cesar worked to help farm workers make a better life for themselves.

In 1952, Chavez joined a group called the Community Service Organization (CSO). Chavez traveled throughout California and made speeches in support of workers' rights. He urged Mexican-Americans to register and vote. He later formed his own organization, the National Farm Workers Association (later called the United Farm Workers). Chavez led strikes against farm owners for higher wages and better working conditions. He also encouraged boycotts to draw the public's attention to the problems of the workers. Until his death in 1993, Cesar Chavez remained active in the fight for the right of all workers to a decent life.

Petition to Farmers

Cesar Chavez and the people who worked with him wanted to be treated fairly by their employers. One way that people can ask for changes is to write a petition, a formal written list of complaints and requests that is signed by many people.

Reread the story and write a list of things that the migrant workers wanted to change. Next to each item listed, write your ideas about why that problem needed to be solved.

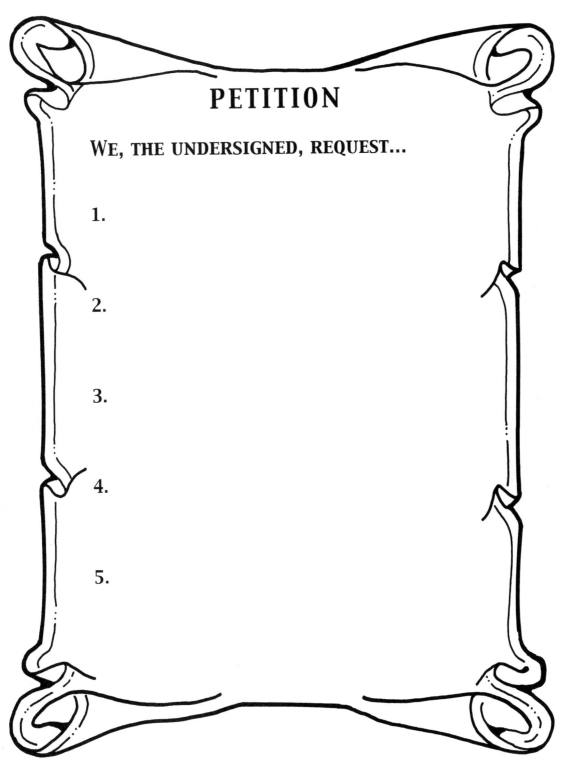

PETITION

WE, THE UNDERSIGNED, REQUEST...

1.

2.

3.

4.

5.

Frederick Douglass
Fairness

Summary

Frederick Douglass, an escaped slave, became an influential leader in the abolition movement. In addition to abolition, he was a strong supporter of women's rights and suffrage for all people. He wrote extensively and gave speeches about fair treatment of people all over the world.

Concepts to Consider

Because of his personal history as well as his place in history, it is easy to think of Frederick Douglass only in terms of his abolition work. Influential as he was in that arena, he was also a strong supporter of fair treatment of all people. He had close ties with the leaders of the women's rights movement in the United States. While in Europe he joined the cause of Irish freedom as well as women's suffrage.

His poised, skillful speaking style led many people to believe he could never have been a slave. Because he was self-educated he was able to convince the world that education would help any person find a more prominent place in the world.

Extended Responses

Discussion Topics

Objective: Students will recognize the significance of Frederick Douglass' education and his accomplishments. They will understand how his influence spread beyond the issues of emancipation and suffrage for Blacks.

• Give examples of how Frederick Douglass' life was changed by his ability to read and write. Could he have accomplished the same things without an education? Support your answer.

• It was against the law for anyone to teach a slave how to read and write. Brainstorm a list of reasons why that law may have been written.

• Frederick Douglass once wrote, "*I am not only an American slave, but a man, and as such, am bound to use my powers for the welfare of the whole human brotherhood.*" Explain what he meant in that statement.

Writing Activity—Page 58

Objective: Students will write a newspaper article that explains and discusses an issue addressed by Frederick Douglass.

On December 3, 1847, the first issue of Frederick Douglass' abolitionist newspaper, *The North Star*, came off the presses. Under different titles, the newspaper continued to run until 1860.

Douglass spoke and wrote on behalf of many causes: education for all, emancipation of the slaves, the rights of freedmen, voting rights for Blacks and for women. On the worksheet "The North Star," students are asked to write a persuasive article on a topic that was addressed by Frederick Douglass in his speaking and writing career.

Frederick Douglass
Fairness

Frederick Douglass was born in February of 1818 on a Maryland plantation. He was separated from his mother when only a few weeks old. He was raised by his grandparents, and only saw his mother four or five times in his entire life. When he was six his grandmother took him to his master's plantation and left him there.

When he was about eight he was sent to Baltimore to live as a houseboy with Hugh and Sophia Auld, relatives of his master. Shortly after his arrival his new mistress taught him the alphabet. Because it was unlawful to teach slaves how to read, her husband made her stop teaching Frederick. But Frederick was determined to learn to read and write. He made the neighborhood boys his teachers, giving away his food in exchange for lessons.

Returning to his master's plantation at the age of fifteen, Douglass became a field hand. He was beaten and starved, but he refused to be discouraged. He was sent to a slavebreaker—a plantation owner known for his ability to tame sullen slaves. Although severely beaten, Douglass refused to be broken. In a final confrontation, the slavebreaker was forced to back down. Douglass' challenge to the slavebreaker restored his sense of self-worth. At about age eighteen, he was sent back to Baltimore to live with the Auld family. While there, he learned how to caulk ships, and in early September, 1838, at the age of twenty, Douglass succeeded in escaping from slavery by impersonating a sailor.

Douglass believed that learning to read and write was a turning point in his own life. As a slave, he taught other slaves to read and write. Throughout his lifetime he took every opportunity to increase his own education. He encouraged all Blacks to take advantage of educational opportunities to build a prominent place for themselves in American society.

He went first to New Bedford, Massachusetts, where he and his new wife Anna Murray began to raise a family. In October, 1841, he spoke at an anti-slavery convention, telling listeners about his life as a slave. His speech was so moving that he was asked to become a lecturer for the Massachusetts Anti-Slavery Society. His speaking tours and writing took him all over the world. He published his own newspaper, *The North Star*. The newspaper's masthead read, "Right is of no sex—Truth is of no color—God is the Father of us all and we are all Brethren."

Douglass participated in the first women's rights convention at Seneca Falls in 1848. He wrote three autobiographies. At his death on February 20, 1895, he was internationally recognized as an abolitionist, an untiring worker for justice and equal opportunity, and an unyielding defender of women's rights.

The North Star

The first issue of Frederick Douglass' abolitionist newspaper, *The North Star*, was printed on December 3, 1847. Douglass spoke and wrote on behalf of fair treatment: education for all, emancipation of the slaves, the rights of freedmen, and voting rights for Blacks and for women. Select one of these topics and write a newspaper article supporting that cause. Include a creative headline for your article.

Dorothea Dix
Caring

Summary

Dorothea Dix led the movement to reform treatment of the mentally ill in the United States. She carried her campaign to Europe. Not only did her achievements gain immediate response, her changes are still being felt today with the way mental patients are treated.

Concepts to Consider

Dorothea Dix was a woman who accomplished much in her lifetime. She was a teacher and then a social reformer for the treatment of the mentally ill. She did not have defined goals, but simply did whatever would best help the people that she saw in need.

There are many circumstances in today's world that cause us concern and cause us to think with sympathy of other people's situations. But it is often difficult to take the next step, which is to help. Talk to students about how even small acts of caring can make an impact on other people's lives.

Extended Responses

Discussion Topics

Objective: Students will recognize how some accomplishments of Dorothea Dix reflect her caring personality.

• Dorothea Dix's schools were "dame schools," schools for girls, taught by women. Many people at that time felt that girls did not need an education. Speculate about what reasons they might have had for thinking that.

• Do you agree with Dorothea Dix's ideas about education? Support your answer.

• During the Civil War, Dorothea was superintendent of the U.S. Army nurses. Why do you think she qualified for this job?

Writing Activity—Page 61

Objective: Students will think of ways they can turn caring feelings into positive action in different areas of their lives.

Because Dorothea Dix was willing to turn her caring into action, she was probably the most effective advocate of humanitarian reform in the 19th century. Even small efforts to act on care or concern about another person can reap tremendous benefits.

The worksheet "From Caring to Action" asks students to think of events or circumstances that they have observed. They are asked to describe each circumstance and propose an action they might take to make it better.

Dorothea Dix
Caring

Dorothea Dix led the drive to build state hospitals for the mentally ill. The effects of the changes she achieved are still evident in the treatment of mentally ill people today.

Dorothea was born in Hampden, Maine, in 1802. Her childhood was difficult. Her father was an alcoholic and her mother suffered from severe headaches and mental illness. From an early age, Dorothea was responsible for the care and education of her two younger brothers. As her parents' behavior became more unstable and abusive, Dorothea and her brothers went to Boston to live with their grandmother, Madame Dix. Dorothea was not happy so she went to live with her aunt for four years.

Dorothea had dreams of being a schoolteacher. She began a dame school for young girls, where she taught for three years. Dorothea returned to Boston, and with her grandmother's support started a school in their home. Her school remained open for 14 years. Then Dorothea was forced to take extended trips to recover from tuberculosis. She returned to Boston in 1841.

In 1841, Dorothea entered East Cambridge Jail to teach a Sunday School class. What she saw there horrified her. Drunks, criminals, and people who were mentally ill were all housed together in unheated, unfurnished, filthy quarters. When she asked authorities why conditions were so bad, she was told that the insane did not feel heat or cold.

Dorothea immediately took her observations to the courts, and after a series of battles, she succeeded in having conditions at the jail improved. From there, she began a round of visits to jails and almshouses where the mentally ill were sent. She took her findings to the Massachusetts legislature, who supported her campaign and expanded the State Hospital for the care of the mentally ill.

Dorothea was revolutionary in thinking that people who were mentally ill would actually benefit from living in clean surroundings with people who cared for them. She would not tolerate the treatment of these people as animals with no feelings or needs.

Dorothea continued her work throughout the eastern half of the United States. Although a request to Congress to set aside land for the help of the mentally ill was vetoed by the President, she played a major role in the founding of 32 mental hospitals, 15 schools for the mentally ill, a school for the blind, and training facilities for nurses. She continued her work in Europe, visiting facilities in England, Scotland, France, Austria, Italy, Greece, Turkey, Russia, Sweden, Denmark, Holland, Belgium, and Germany. Dorothea never married, and as she neared the end of life, she retired to the mental hospital in New Jersey, the first she had opened. Dorothea died on July 17, 1887.

From Caring to Action

Dorothea Dix not only cared about the people she saw and met, she turned her caring into action and did something to make things better. How many chances do you have to do that in your own life? Think of situations you see or hear about every day, at home, at school, when you're in a public place, or on the news. Describe a situation and propose a caring solution to a problem you see in each place.

At Home	**At School**

In a Public Place **(library, mall, downtown)**	**On the News**

Mother Teresa
Caring

Story Summary

Mother Teresa left her religious community in Calcutta, India to live and work among the poor and sick people in the city's streets. Her mission to help the needy one-on-one has grown into a worldwide charity movement.

Concepts to Consider

Mother Teresa was awarded the Nobel Peace Prize in 1979. She did not want to accept it, but was finally persuaded to accept it on behalf of the people she worked for. To her, it was a reminder to the world of "…the hungry, the naked, the homeless, of the crippled, of the blind, of the lepers, of all those people who feel unwanted, unloved, uncared-for throughout society…"

Lead students to discuss the difference between simple charity and devoting oneself to working one-on-one with people in need. Ask them for suggestions about how this can be carried out in their own lives.

Extended Responses

Discussion Topics

Objective: Students will examine different words that are related to "caring," and draw conclusions about how the words reflect different levels of feeling.

- Mother Teresa once said, "The poor do not need our sympathy and our pity. The poor need our love and compassion." Use a dictionary to define the words *sympathy, pity, love,* and *compassion.*

- Compare and contrast the definitions of the words. Explain how *love* and *compassion* are different from *sympathy* and *pity.*

Writing Activity—Page 64

Objective: Students will create visual reminders to help them change sympathetic or caring feelings into actions.

To be a caring person means more than just having sympathetic feelings about the hardships of others. It is important to act on these feelings if you want to change things for the better.

The worksheet "Caring Reminders" gives students an opportunity to think of their own statements reminding them to help people by doing. Motivational cards could be taped to desktops or inside notebooks, or displayed on a character education bulletin board.

Mother Teresa
Caring

Mother Teresa, born Agnes Bojaxhiu, was born in Yugoslavia on August 27, 1910. Her father was a farmer. She had her first thoughts of doing religious work at age 11. As a teen, she decided to train for missionary work in India. When she was 18 she left home to join the Sisters of Lareto, an Irish religious community with a mission in Calcutta, India. She trained for a few months in Dublin, then was sent to India. In 1928, she took her vows in India.

From 1929 to 1948, Mother Teresa taught at St. Mary's High School in Calcutta, but the suffering and poverty she saw outside the convent walls made a deep impression on her. In 1946, she received permission from her superiors to leave the convent school and devote herself to working among the poor in the slums of Calcutta.

Mother Teresa did not want to just work among the poor. She wanted to live among them. She went to another community to take nursing training, her first step toward her goal. She came back to Calcutta and started to visit the homes of the poor, talking to them, washing babies, and offering medical help. Mother Teresa found the means to provide the people with medicine, clothes, and food. She established a place where the poor could come for the help they needed. She had no home, but slept with the Sisters of the Poor. Although she had no funds, she started an open-air school for homeless children.

Soon she was joined by voluntary helpers, and financial support came from various church organizations as well as from the city officials. This made it possible for her to extend the scope of her work. On October 7, 1950, she received permission to start her own order, The Missionaries of Charity. The order's primary task was to love and care for those people nobody was prepared to look after. Today the order is made up of nearly one thousand sisters and brothers in India. Many have been trained as doctors, nurses, and social workers. They are in a position to provide effective help for the slum population as well as doing relief work in connection with natural catastrophes like floods, epidemics, famine, and swarms of refugees.

Before her death in 1997, Mother Teresa had at least fifty relief projects operating in India. These include work among slum-dwellers, children's homes, homes for the dying, clinics, and a leper colony. Her order has also spread to other countries in Africa, Asia, and Latin America, as well as Italy, Great Britain, Ireland, and the United States.

Motivational Cards

"Show You Care by Doing" is a good motto for anyone to live by. Create some motivational cards to help remind yourself that caring with actions will make your worl a better place. Think of your own motivational sayings or reminders. Write them in the cards below. Cut out the cards and place them in places where you will see them.

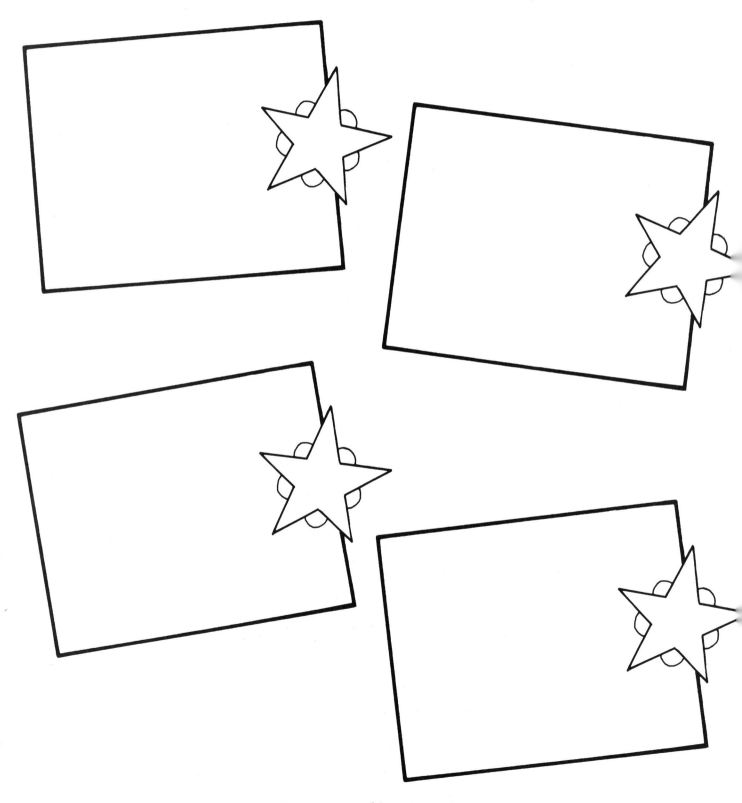